CW01476344

Take Courage

Eight Lessons from Men of Faith

Andy Sochor

Gospel Armory
PUBLISHING

Take Courage: Eight Lessons from Men of Faith
Copyright © 2014 by Andy Sochor

Published by:
Gospel Armory Publishing
Bowling Green, Kentucky
www.GospelArmory.com

Printed in the United States of America

ISBN: 978-1-942036-02-9

Table of Contents

"The wicked flee when no one is pursuing,
but the righteous are bold as a lion."
Proverbs 28:1

Introduction

In concluding His final address to the apostles before His arrest, Jesus told them to be courageous in the face of the hardships that would be coming against them.

> "*These things I have spoken to you, so that in Me you may have peace. In the world you have tribulation, but take courage; I have overcome the world*" (John 16:33).

Courage is the confidence and conviction to do what one knows to be right, regardless of the consequences. The apostles needed *courage* to carry out the Lord's instructions without being deterred by the persecution that awaited them.

As Christians, we also need to have *courage* today. The Lord has left instructions for us to follow. We are to "*observe all that* [Christ] *commanded*" (Matthew 28:20). Furthermore, we are warned that we will become targets by following the Lord's instructions. Paul said, "*Indeed, all who desire to live godly in Christ Jesus will be persecuted*" (2 Timothy 3:12).

So how can we "*take courage*" (John 16:33) so that we will be able to endure the sufferings that will come for the cause of Christ? This is the question we will seek to answer in our study. The lessons that follow will focus on examples from the Old Testament of men who displayed courage in their particular circumstances. From these examples, we will learn how to be courageous in the face of various challenges of life. But in this first lesson, will address the question in more general terms. How do we "*take courage*" today?

We Must Know What is Right

There are many people who display courage in standing for beliefs which they hold in error. While we certainly need courage, we must also understand that all the courage in the world will not change what is false to what is true. Therefore, if we are going to have the courage to do what we know to be right, we first need to be sure that we *know what is right*.

Truth is found in the word of God. When Jesus prayed to the Father, He said, "*Sanctify them in the truth; Your word is truth*" (John 17:17). The psalmist wrote, "*The sum of Your word is truth*" (Psalm 119:160). The first step to taking courage must be to learn and become convinced of the truth of God's word so that we might be "*established in the truth*" (2 Peter 1:12). This will not happen for us miraculously or by some accident, but by diligent study of the Scriptures (2 Timothy 2:15).

We Must Know There is a Reward

Once we are convinced of the truth, we must have a reason for "*holding fast* [to] *the word of life*" (Philippians 2:16). The only thing that makes suffering for the truth bearable is the hope of the resurrection to eternal life. Without this hope, Paul said, "*We are of all men most to be pitied*" (1 Corinthians 15:19). Without this hope, the truth is not worth standing for.

But there is hope for life after death. Paul wrote, *"But now Christ has been raised from the dead, the first fruits of those who are asleep"* (1 Corinthians 15:20). The resurrection of Christ gives us hope of being raised ourselves. But this hope is not for a resurrection leading to a new life in the same world in which we currently live. We have *"a living hope through the resurrection of Jesus Christ from the dead, to obtain an inheritance which is imperishable and undefiled and will not fade away, reserved in heaven..."* (1 Peter 1:3-4). The promise of heaven shows us that the truth is worth standing for, allowing us to *take courage*.

We Must Act

It is not enough to know the truth and to be convinced of the promised reward. Having *courage* means we must act according to what we know to be true. Having courage means we will *"live godly in Christ Jesus,"* even if it means we *"will be persecuted"* (2 Timothy 3:12). Having courage means we will *"keep [our] behavior excellent,"* even though others may *"slander [us] as evildoers"* (1 Peter 2:12). Having courage means we will *"do"* what Jesus commanded, even it it means that *"the world hates"* us (John 15:14, 18). Having courage means we will *"not run with [the ungodly] into the same excesses of dissipation,"* even it if means *"they malign"* us (1 Peter 4:4). Having courage means we will *"preach the word... in season and out of season,"* even if those we try to teach *"will not endure sound doctrine"* (2 Timothy 4:2-3). Having courage means we will *"be faithful until death,"* even if it means having to endure *"tribulation"* (Revelation 2:10).

As we get into specific examples in the lessons to follow, we will see what the men of old did in order to display courage. They did not just *know* and *believe* the truth. They did what they knew to be pleasing to God, even though they had to endure challenges and suffering for it.

Conclusion

As disciples of Christ, we must *take courage* so that we might continually please our Lord regardless of the consequences. This means we must learn what is right, recognize and appreciate the reward, and then do what we know to be right.

Remember the assurance that Jesus gave His apostles: *"Take courage; I have overcome the world"* (John 16:33). No matter what trials or tribulations we may have to face, Paul provided the reminder to us that *"we overwhelmingly conquer through Him who loved us"* (Romans 8:37). So take courage! Do what is right no matter what the consequences may be in this life. Jesus overcame the world. We can overcome and gain eternal life through Him.

Questions for Discussion & Reflection

1. Define courage.

2. Why is it important for Christians to have courage today?

3. Explain why it is necessary to know what is right in order to properly display courage.

4. What is it that ought to motivate us to take courage?

5. After we know what is right and understand the proper motivation for taking courage, what is the final step in living a life of courage?

6. What has Jesus done that allows us to be able to take courage?

Abram
The Courage to Leave Home

The first example we will consider in this series is Abram. He displayed courage when God called him to leave home and go to an unknown land which the Lord would show to him.

> *"Now the Lord said to Abram, 'Go forth from your country, and from your relatives and from your father's house, to the land which I will show you; and I will make you a great nation, and I will bless you, and make your name great; and so you shall be a blessing; and I will bless those who bless you, and the one who curses you I will curse. And in you all the families of the earth will be blessed.'*

> *"So Abram went forth as the Lord had spoken to him; and Lot went with him. Now Abram was seventy-five years old when he departed from Haran. Abram took Sarai his wife and Lot his nephew, and all their possessions which they had accumulated, and the persons which they had acquired in Haran, and they set out for the land of Canaan; thus they came to the land of Canaan"* (Genesis 12:1-5).

God is not going to speak to us today and tell us to leave our home like He did with Abram. But there are lessons about acting with *courage* to be learned from Abram's example. Courage is *faithfulness* in the midst of trials and temptations. In the example of Abram, we see one who sacrificed what was comfortable and familiar for hardship and uncertainty.

The Background

Abram left Ur with his wife, father, and nephew and settled in Haran (Genesis 11:31). The text says, *"They went out together from Ur of the Chaldeans in order to enter the land of Canaan"* (Genesis 11:31). Yet the inspired record indicates that they stopped and settled in Haran. Terah, Abram's father, would later die in Haran before any of his family ever reached Canaan (Genesis 11:32).

After he and his family settled in Haran, God called Abram to leave. What was he to leave? God said, *"Go forth from your country, and from your relatives and from your father's house"* (Genesis 12:1). He was called to go to a land which God would show him (Genesis 12:1). The Lord assured Abram that he would be blessed (Genesis 12:2).

When God called, Abram obeyed (Genesis 12:4-5). He left with his wife, Lot, and all of their possessions. This occurred when Abram was already seventy-five years old (Genesis 12:4). As we will see later in this lesson, his age was significant.

Why This Took Courage

The Scriptures provide a few reasons why it took *courage* for Abram to leave his home and follow where the Lord would lead him.

First, it took courage because he did not know where he was going. The text states that Abram and his family left Ur *"in order to enter the land of Canaan"* (Genesis 11:31), but there is no indication that Abram had any familiarity with the land when God called him. As a matter of history, we know that Abram was going to the land of Canaan. But Abram left Haran *"not knowing where he was going"* (Hebrews 11:8). Familiarity with an area would allow one to plan the best route and prepare for specific challenges he would face. Abram did not have this luxury. Instead he simply put his faith in God and followed the Lord.

Second, it took courage because he had to leave his father and his relatives. This was the time of the Patriarchs. One's identity was tied to his family. While he was alive, the patriarch was the head of the generations that followed. Abram was told to leave his *"relatives"* and his *"father's house"* (Genesis 12:1). He was divorcing himself from his kinsmen during a time when one had to rely on these people for support, protection, and companionship. Furthermore, Abram did this when he was *"seventy-five years old"* (Genesis 12:4) – hardly a young man eager to move out on his own. He had ties to his family that were firmly established over the course of decades. But he left his family so that he might become the *"friend of God"* (James 2:23).

Third, it took courage because he had to leave the home he had established for himself in Haran. Again, Abram was seventy-five years old when God called him (Genesis 12:4). Yes, people generally lived longer then, but he was still not far from *"old age"* (Genesis 21:2). This description was used when Abram was *"one hundred years old"* (Genesis 21:5). He left with no guarantee that he would ever get settled again. But he was seeking God's reward. The Hebrew writer said, *"By faith he lived as an alien in the land of promise, as in a foreign land, dwelling in tents...for he was looking for a city which has foundations, whose architect and builder is God"* (Hebrews 11:9-10).

Abram Took Courage

Abram knew what was right. God *told* him what to do: *"Go forth...to the land which I will show you"* (Genesis 12:1). He responded *"by faith"* (Hebrews 11:8). Abram *knew* what was right because God revealed it to him. The only way *anyone* can know what is right in the sight of God is through the Spirit's revelation to man (1 Corinthians 2:10-12).

More than simply knowing what was right, Abram believed in God's promises. God promised to make of him *"a great nation"* and that through his seed *"all the families of the earth* [would] *be blessed"* (Genesis 12:2-3). Though Abram was childless, God promised him descendants; and he believed (Genesis 15:5-6). Because of this belief, Abram became the father of the faithful (Romans 4:3, 11).

After knowing God's instructions and believing in His promises, Abram acted. God told him, *"Go forth"* (Genesis 12:1). Without hesitation, *"Abram went forth as the Lord had spoken to him"* (Genesis 12:4). *"When he was called,* [he] *obeyed"* (Hebrews 11:8), even though it meant being a stranger in the promised land (Hebrews 11:9). Acting according to God's instructions was a sign of courage on the part of Abram.

Application for Us

God is not directly calling us to leave our homeland and relatives today. But there are certainly lessons for us to learn from the example of Abram.

First, we must be willing to follow God wherever He calls us to go. Again, the calling is different, but we are certainly called. Paul said that we are "*called...through* [the] *gospel*" (2 Thessalonians 2:14). Being called through the gospel does not mean we simply hear the word and believe in God's promises. Many believe that such a response to the gospel is sufficient for salvation. But the example of Abram shows us that salvation is "*not by faith alone*" (James 2:20-24). If we "*do not obey the gospel,*" we will "*pay the penalty of eternal destruction*" (2 Thessalonians 1:8-9). Jesus is "*to all those who obey Him the source of eternal salvation*" (Hebrews 5:9). If we want to be saved, we must obey the instructions found in His word. As Mary told the servants at the wedding feast, "*Whatever He says to you, do it*" (John 2:5).

Second, we must be willing to put God above our family. Jesus said, "*Do not think that I came to bring peace on the earth; I did not come to bring peace, but a sword. For I came to set a man against His father, and a daughter against her mother, and a daughter-in-law against her mother-in-law; and a man's enemies will be the members of his household. He who loves father or mother more than Me is not worthy of Me; and he who loves son or daughter more than Me is not worthy of Me*" (Matthew 10:34-37). If forsaking family in order to follow Christ is necessary, we must do it. Would this be difficult? Sure it would. But we must put the Lord above everyone – even those who are the closest to us in this life.

Third, we must recognize that we are strangers on the earth. But more than just acknowledging this status, we must act like we are strangers. Peter wrote, *"Beloved, I urge you as aliens and strangers to abstain from fleshly lusts which wage war against the soul"* (1 Peter 2:11). We must *"not be conformed to this world, but transformed"* (Romans 12:2). Remember that *"our citizenship is in heaven"* (Philippians 3:20). Abram's desire was to find *"the city which has foundations whose architect and builder is God"* (Hebrews 11:10). He desired *"a better country, that is, a heavenly one"* (Hebrews 11:16). This must be our desire as well.

Conclusion

Abram was willing to leave what was comfortable and familiar in order to follow the Lord. We must be willing to sacrifice anything – even our own lives (Romans 12:1) – so that we might please the Lord. It will not be easy, but we must *take courage* and do it.

Questions for Discussion & Reflection

1. How does God call us today?

2. Abram was the father of the faithful. What does his example teach us about faith? (See Hebrews 11:8)

3. Describe the circumstances that would require us to choose between God and our family.

4. Why does it take courage to forsake family in order to follow Christ?

5. If we are strangers on earth, how should that affect our behavior?

6. As Christians, where is our citizenship?

Joseph
The Courage to Maintain Purity

The second example in our study is Joseph. He had the courage to maintain purity when he was tempted to compromise his morals. When his master's wife seduced him, this young man refused to yield, choosing instead to act in such a way that would please God.

"It came about after these events that his master's wife looked with desire at Joseph, and she said, 'Lie with me.' But he refused and said to his master's wife, 'Behold, with me here, my master does not concern himself with anything in the house, and he has put all that he owns in my charge. There is no one greater in this house than I, and he has withheld nothing from me except you, because you are his wife. How then could I do this great evil and sin against God?'

"As she spoke to Joseph day after day, he did not listen to her to lie beside her or be with her. Now it happened one day that he went into the house to do his work, and none of the men of the household was there inside. She caught him by his garment, saying, 'Lie with me!' And he left his garment in her hand and fled, and went outside" (Genesis 39:7-12).

We live in a society in which immorality is common – premarital sex, adultery, homosexuality, pornography. We need to have the *courage* to maintain our purity "*in the midst of a crooked and perverse generation*" (Philippians 2:15). Joseph's example shows us how to do this.

The Background

Joseph was the favored son of his father. "*Israel loved Joseph more than all his sons, because he was the son of his old age; and he made him a varicolored tunic*" (Genesis 37:3). Though the parent is to blame when such favoritism is shown, the resentment by the siblings is usually directed toward the favored child. This was what happened in the case of Joseph. "*His brothers saw that their father loved him more than all his brothers; and so they hated him and could not speak to him on friendly terms*" (Genesis 37:4).

Joseph's brothers hated him even more for his dreams. In one dream, Joseph's sheaf rose up while his brothers' sheaves bowed down to his (Genesis 37:5-7). The brothers knew exactly what this meant: "'*Are you actually going to reign over us? Or are you really going to rule over us?*' *So they hated him even more for his dreams and for his words*" (Genesis 37:8). Their problem was that they understood the meaning without recognizing that the dream came from God. The second dream was similar. The sun, moon, and eleven stars bowed down to him, signifying that his brothers and parents would all bow down before him (Genesis 37:9-11).

After these dreams, Joseph was sent by his father to check on his brothers who were pasturing the flock in the area of Shechem (Genesis 37:12-13). When his brothers saw him, they planned to take advantage of this opportunity to kill Joseph (Genesis 37:18-20). After Reuben intervened and convinced the brothers to throw him in a pit instead – with the plan that he would come back later and rescue Joseph – the other brothers decided to sell Joseph to some traders that were passing by (Genesis 37:21-28). These traders *"brought Joseph into Egypt"* and *"sold him in Egypt to Potiphar, Pharaoh's officer, the captain of the bodyguard"* (Genesis 37:28,36). While he was serving Potiphar, he was tempted to commit fornication with his master's wife.

Why This Took Courage

Given his circumstances, there are at least five reasons why it took *courage* for Joseph to maintain purity and resist the temptations of Potiphar's wife.

First, the temptation was to fulfill a natural desire which God had instilled in man. God created man in such a way that he would desire sexual gratification. However, just because such a desire was given by God does not mean that man has the license to fulfill that desire in any way he pleases. The Hebrew writer said, *"Marriage is to be held in honor among all, and the marriage bed is to be undefiled; for fornicators and adulterers God will judge"* (Hebrews 13:4). It would have been natural for Joseph, as a young man, to have the desire for sexual gratification. Yet it would have been sinful to fulfill that desire with another man's wife (Genesis 39:9).

Second, Joseph was the only God-fearing person in this area. The Egyptians certainly were religious, but they did not serve the true and living God. Those who believed in God sold him into slavery. Joseph could have turned against God because of them. He could have reasoned that there was no point in following God when no one else there was following Him. We are reminded in the example of Peter that it is much easier to boldly proclaim one's faith when among like-minded friends (Matthew 26:33-35) than it is to do so when one is standing alone among those in the world (Matthew 26:69-75).

Third, the temptation was regular and persistent. Potiphar's wife did not just tempt Joseph one time and then leave him alone after he refused her advances. "*As she spoke to Joseph day after day, he did not listen to her to lie beside her or be with her*" (Genesis 39:10). Continual temptation like this often wears someone down to the point in which he gives in to sins he once resisted.

Fourth, Joseph may have been able to sin without others finding out. After the temptations had been going on for some time, an opportunity presented itself in which Joseph might have been able to give in without anyone else knowing. "*Now it happened one day that he went into the house to do his work, and none of the men of the household was there inside. She caught him by his garment, saying, 'Lie with me!'*" (Genesis 39:11-12). No one was home except Joseph and Potiphar's wife. This would have been the ideal time to commit fornication with her without anyone else knowing about it.

Fifth, the temptation had reached the point in which Joseph could no longer just say "no." At the final temptation, the situation had become such that a simple "no" would no longer be sufficient. She had "*caught him by his garment*" (Genesis 39:12). He could have said "no" and she would have still been there clinging to his clothes. More was needed to resist this temptation. So "*he left his garment in her hand and fled*" (Genesis 39:12).

Joseph Took Courage

Joseph knew what was right. He knew that it would be wrong to give in to Potiphar's wife's temptations. Why? First, it would betray the trust of his master: "*Behold, with me here, my master does not concern himself with anything in the house, and he has put all that he owns in my charge. There is no one greater in this house than I, and he has withheld nothing from me except you, because you are his wife*" (Genesis 39:8-9). Second, and more importantly, it would be a "*sin against God*" (Genesis 39:9).

Joseph also believed that God would bless him for doing what was right. He already had the dreams that indicated God's plan to exalt him (Genesis 37:5-11). He did not want to sin *against* God (Genesis 39:9), which implies a fear of divine judgment. Even though he was separated from his people, he wanted to be sure he was still in God's favor.

Finally, at the critical time of temptation, Joseph acted. When Potiphar's wife first tempted him, he refused (Genesis 39:7-9). When she persisted day after day, he remained steadfast (Genesis 39:10). When the situation escalated, he fled (Genesis 39:12).

Application for Us

Joseph's example provides several lessons for us.

First, we must maintain sexual purity in order to please God. We are to respect God's arrangement for fulfilling these natural desires – marriage (Hebrews 13:4; 1 Corinthians 7:1-2). But even without marriage, we must resist temptation (1 Corinthians 10:13). When Paul wrote to Timothy – a young, unmarried man – he told him to treat *"younger women as sisters, in all purity"* (1 Timothy 5:2). He was not to flirt with sin and see how close he could get to it.

Second, we must be faithful to God, even if we must stand alone. Though he would later deny Jesus, Peter's initial attitude was commendable: *"Even though all may fall away because of You, I will never fall away"* (Matthew 26:33). If brethren forsake, desert, or mistreat us, it is discouraging; but we must remain faithful anyway (2 Timothy 4:16-17).

Third, we must remain steadfast, even if temptation is persistent. Peter warned his readers: *"Be on your guard so that you are not carried away by the error of unprincipled men and fall from your own steadfastness"* (2 Peter 3:17). It is possible for one to be steadfast but eventually give in to error and sin and fall away.

Fourth, we must avoid sin, even if we think no one will find out. Even if it might be possible to sin with no other human being aware of our transgression, God will know. *"And there is no creature hidden from His sight, but all things are open and laid bare to the eyes of Him with whom we have to do"* (Hebrews 4:13).

Fifth, when necessary, we must be willing to *flee* temptation. Paul said, *"Flee immorality"* (1 Corinthians 6:18), and, *"Flee from youthful lusts"* (2 Timothy 2:22). This does not necessarily mean we must *run* as Joseph did. But it does mean that we *leave* any situation that poses a great threat and temptation for us – whether it be a friendship, job, city, etc.

Conclusion

Joseph maintained purity even though he was forsaken by those who should have supported him and was severely tempted to commit a sin that would have been difficult for many young men to resist. We must diligently strive to keep *"the marriage bed...undefiled"* (Hebrews 13:4). Then when we are tempted to seek sexual gratification outside of this divinely-approved arrangement, we must ask what Joseph asked: *"How then could I do this great evil and sin against God?"*

Questions for Discussion & Reflection

1. When Joseph refused the advances of Potiphar's wife, he was ultimately refusing to sin against whom?

2. What arrangement has God provided for us to fulfill natural sexual desires?

3. How can one who is unmarried maintain sexual purity?

4. Why are persistent temptations dangerous?

5. Even if we manage to hide our sin from everyone else, who will always know about it?

6. Explain why it might be necessary to flee from certain temptations.

Moses

The Courage to Lead

Moses was chosen by God to lead the Israelites out of the land of Egypt. At first he was hesitant to do this. But in the end, Moses obeyed the Lord, stood against Pharaoh, and led the people out of bondage and toward the promised land.

> *"The Lord said, 'I have surely seen the affliction of My people who are in Egypt, and have given heed to their cry because of their taskmasters, for I am aware of their sufferings. So I have come down to deliver them from the power of the Egyptians, and to bring them up from that land to a good and spacious land, to a land flowing with milk and honey, to the place of the Canaanite and the Hittite and the Amorite and the Perizzite and the Hivite and the Jebusite. Now, behold, the cry of the sons of Israel has come to Me; furthermore, I have seen the oppression with which the Egyptians are oppressing them. Therefore, come now, and I will send you to Pharaoh, so that you may bring My people, the sons of Israel, out of Egypt'"* (Exodus 3:7-10).

We often associate *leading* with *leadership roles* (husbands, employers, generals, Presidents, elders, etc.). But we can also lead without an official leadership position.

Leadership can be exerted through one's position, words, actions, and influence. We lead by directing others toward the way they should go and by showing them how to do what is right. There are ways in which each of us can *lead* within the roles we occupy (in the church, home, workplace, society, etc.). But it takes *courage* to do so. Moses is an example of one who had the *courage* to lead.

The Background

The children of Israel settled in Egypt in order to survive a famine (Genesis 45:5-8; 47:11-12). Thanks to Joseph (Genesis 47:11-12) – with the help of God (Genesis 45:5, 7) – they prospered. *"Now Israel lived in the land of Egypt, in Goshen, and they acquired property in it and were fruitful and became very numerous"* (Genesis 47:27).

All of this happened while Pharaoh thought highly of Joseph (Genesis 41:39-45; 45:16-20). However, eventually *"a new king arose over Egypt, who did not know Joseph"* (Exodus 1:8). He saw the Israelites as a threat (Exodus 1:9-10), so he tried to keep them under his control by making *"their lives bitter with hard labor"* (Exodus 1:11-14).

However, God was with the Israelites and blessed them (Exodus 1:12). Even still, their oppression was severe. They *"cried out"*; *"God heard their groaning; and God remembered His covenant with Abraham, Isaac, and Jacob. God saw the sons of Israel, and God took notice of them"* (Exodus 2:23-25). So He planned to deliver the Israelites out of bondage (Exodus 3:7-9). He chose Moses to lead them (Exodus 3:10).

Why This Took Courage

When we consider the example of Moses, we can find five reasons why it took *courage* for him to lead the people out of Egypt.

First, Moses did not aspire to lead. Some people are natural born leaders. Others simply want to be in charge. Moses was not like this. When God called him to lead he tried to come up with excuses so that he would not have to do it. He saw himself as being unfit to stand up to Pharaoh (Exodus 3:11). He was afraid that the Israelites would not listen to him (Exodus 4:1). He claimed to be a poor speaker (Exodus 4:10). Eventually he said, *"Please, Lord, now send the message by whomever You will"* (Exodus 4:13). He wanted God to send *anyone* but him.

Second, Moses had to face opposition. He first had to face Pharaoh – the leader of the most powerful nation on earth at that time (Exodus 3:11; 5:1-2). At one point Pharaoh threatened to kill him (Exodus 10:28). When Moses finally did lead the people out of Egypt, Pharaoh and his army pursued them (Exodus 14:9). If this were not enough, he also faced opposition from his brethren (Exodus 5:20-21), from Miriam and Aaron (Numbers 12:1-2), and from Korah and his allies (Numbers 16:1-3).

Third, the people often did not want to follow. When Pharaoh pursued them, they said, *"It is because there were no graves in Egypt that you have taken us away to die in the wilderness? Why have you dealt with us in this way, bringing us out of Egypt? Is this not the word that we spoke to you in Egypt, saying, 'Leave us alone that we may serve the Egyptians'? For it would have been better for us to serve the Egyptians than to die in the wilderness*" (Exodus 14:11-12). This was not the only time the Israelites wished they had never left Egypt (Exodus 16:3; 17:3; Numbers 11:5-6; 14:2-3). At one point they even wanted to "*appoint* [another] *leader and return to Egypt*" (Numbers 14:4).

Fourth, Moses had to lead the people out of comfort, security, and prosperity. Moses was leading them from bondage into a state of freedom and blessings from God. This may not seem like it would be hard to convince the people to follow for this, but it is – it demands a strong faith in God and a firm sense of personal responsibility. People often accept oppression if it allows them to be dependent. This is what happened with the Israelites. Though they were sorely oppressed by Pharaoh, they preferred to "*serve the Egyptians*" (Exodus 14:2) if it meant they were able to eat "*bread to the full*" (Exodus 16:3; cf. Numbers 11:4-6). Moses had to lead them away from the free food provided by their oppressive leaders to the blessings provided by the God of heaven.

Fifth, Moses had to lead in the right way. He was not to be an oppressive leader like the ruler of Egypt – even though at one point in his life he was potentially positioned to attain that role (Exodus 2:10; Hebrews 11:24-26). He led as God's chosen spokesman (Exodus 7:1-2).

Moses Took Courage

Moses knew what was right. God spoke directly to him (Exodus 3:6) and told him what he needed to do – lead the people of Israel out of Egypt (Exodus 3:7-8, 10, 14-17).

Moses believed that he would be rewarded for heeding God's call. The Hebrew writer tells us that he considered *"the reproach of Christ greater riches than the treasures of Egypt; for he was looking to the reward"* (Hebrews 11:26).

Finally, Moses took courage and put his faith into action. He confronted Pharaoh and delivered God's message: *"Let My people go"* (Exodus 5:1). Stephen said of Moses, *"This man led* [the people] *out"* of the land of Egypt (Acts 7:36).

Application for Us

Though we may not lead God's people away from an oppressive ruler and into a land flowing with milk and honey, there are applications to be made from the example of Moses.

First, we must be willing to do things we may not be comfortable doing. Before Jesus performed his first miracle at a wedding feast in Cana, his mother told the servants, *"Whatever He says to you, do it"* (John 2:5). We need to follow this same instruction. We must do *whatever* – not just what we might be comfortable with – the Lord instructs us to do in His word (Matthew 28:18-20; Hebrews 5:9).

Second, we must be able to stand up to opposition. Paul warned the Ephesian elders that opposition to the truth may come from two directions. There may be *"savage wolves"* who *"will come in among you"* (Acts 20:29). There may also be men *"from among your own selves"* who will try to lead Christians away from the truth (Acts 20:30). Being among brethren is not justification for us to let our guard down. We must be ready to face opposition from wherever it may come.

Third, we must try to lead and influence people, even if they do not want to follow. Jesus was *"the Light* [that] *has come into the world,"* but many refused to *"come to the Light for fear that* [their] *deeds* [would] *be exposed"* (John 3:19-20). We also *"appear as lights in the world"* (Philippians 2:15; cf. Matthew 5:14-16). Because of this, many will oppose us just as they did with Moses and Jesus (cf. John 15:18-19).

Fourth, we must promote freedom in Christ over dependence upon the enemies of Christ. Jesus offers us freedom (John 8:31-32; 2 Corinthians 3:17). But just as the freedom proclaimed by Moses required a strong faith in God and a sense of personal responsibility, proclaiming freedom in Christ today demands the same – faith in God and His reward (Hebrews 6:11-12) and personal responsibility for our salvation (Philippians 2:12).

Fifth, we must lead as God would have us to lead. We cannot try to force people to comply as a wicked ruler like Pharaoh would. We must lead others through words (1 Peter 4:11), actions (1 Peter 2:12), and by fulfilling whatever divinely-approved leadership role we may occupy (Romans 12:8).

Conclusion

Moses had many excuses for *not* leading the children of Israel out of Egypt. Yet he proved himself to be a man of courage by carrying out the difficult task of leading a reluctant people away from the bondage of a godless tyrant. Though we may not have as great of a burden of leadership as Moses had, we all have the opportunity to lead people in one way or another – whether it is through an official leadership position or through the influence we exert over those around us. It may be tempting to make excuses as Moses did. But let us *take courage* and lead in a way that would be pleasing to God.

Questions for Discussion & Reflection

1. How might one lead without being in an official leadership role?

2. Explain the importance of going beyond our comfort zone in our service to God.

3. When Paul spoke with the Ephesian elders, what did he warn were the two directions from which opposition to the truth would come?

4. Will everyone that we try to lead to the truth be willing to follow? Why or why not?

5. Why might some not find freedom in Christ appealing?

6. Rather than leading by force, how does God expect us to
   lead others?

David

The Courage to Fight

The next example in our series is David who had the courage to fight. There are several examples in David's life of him courageously fighting against his enemies (and God's enemies). But for our lesson, we will focus on his fight against the Philistine giant, Goliath.

> *"Then a champion came out from the armies of the Philistines named Goliath, from Gath, whose height was six cubits and a span. He had a bronze helmet on his head, and he was clothed with scale-armor which weighed five thousand shekels of bronze. He also had bronze greaves on his legs and a bronze javelin slung between his shoulders. The shaft of his spear was like a weaver's beam, and the head of his spear weighed six hundred shekels of iron; his shield-carrier also walked before him.*

> *"He stood and shouted to the ranks of Israel and said to them, 'Why do you come out to draw up in battle array? Am I not the Philistine and you servants of Saul? Choose a man for yourselves and let him come down to me. If he is able to fight with me and kill me, then we will become your servants; but if I prevail against him and kill him, then you shall become our servants and serve us.' Again the*

Philistine said, 'I defy the ranks of Israel this day; give me a man that we may fight together.' When Saul and all Israel heard these words of the Philistine, they were dismayed and greatly afraid" (1 Samuel 17:4-11).

"David said to Saul, 'Let no man's heart fail on account of him; your servant will go and fight with this Philistine'" (1 Samuel 17:32).

The nature of our fight today may be different. Paul said, *"For though we walk in the flesh, we do not war according to the flesh, for the weapons of our warfare are not of the flesh, but divinely powerful for the destruction of fortresses. We are destroying speculations and every lofty thing raised up against the knowledge of God, and we are taking every thought captive to the obedience of Christ"* (2 Corinthians 10:3-5). Even so, there are still valuable lessons for us to learn from David's fight against Goliath.

The Background

Saul, the first king of Israel, had just been *"rejected"* by God *"from being king"* because of his failure to obey the Lord and destroy the Amalekites (1 Samuel 15:22-23). Once God rejected Saul, He sent Samuel to Bethlehem to anoint a new king – a son of Jesse (1 Samuel 16:1). The seven older sons of Jesse passed before Samuel, but God did not choose one of them (1 Samuel 16:10). Instead, God chose David – the youngest who was initially excluded from this gathering and left out tending the sheep (1 Samuel 16:11-13). Yet he was God's choice to succeed Saul. So Samuel *"anointed him in the midst of his brothers"* (1 Samuel 16:13).

Later, Israel assembled to do battle with the Philistines (1 Samuel 17:1-3). Goliath, a giant and valiant warrior, issued a challenge to the Israelites – a one-on-one, winner take all duel between himself and anyone the Israelites chose to represent them (1 Samuel 17:4-10). Saul should have answered the challenge. One of the reasons why the people of Israel wanted a king in the first place was so that he would "*go out before* [them] *and fight* [their] *battles*" (1 Samuel 8:20). Besides this, Saul was "*taller than any of the people from his shoulders upward*" (1 Samuel 10:23). But Saul was like the rest of his people – "*dismayed and greatly afraid*" (1 Samuel 17:11).

David's three older brothers were in the army, and his father sent him to deliver provisions and bring back a report on their welfare (1 Samuel 17:10, 17-19). While there, David found out about Goliath's challenge and the reward for defeating him (1 Samuel 17:25-27). Even though his oldest brother mocked and ridiculed him (1 Samuel 17:28), David volunteered to fight (1 Samuel 17:32). Initially, Saul was hesitant to let him go; but David was confident that he would win (1 Samuel 17:33-37). After refusing the king's sword and armor, David took his sling and gathered five smooth stones on his way to face Goliath (1 Samuel 17:38-40).

When David came to fight, Goliath mocked him (1 Samuel 17:41-44). David responded by declaring his confidence that "*the Lord* [would] *deliver* [Goliath] *into* [his] *hands*" (1 Samuel 17:45-47). With one stone, David killed the giant, then cut off the warrior's head with his own sword (1 Samuel 17:48-51). This led to a great victory by the Israelites over the Philistines (1 Samuel 17:52-53).

Why This Took Courage

It is easy to see that it took *courage* for David to fight Goliath. Let us notice four reasons why this was such a courageous act.

First, David was a youth. This was Saul's first reason for discouraging David from going: *"You are not able to go against this Philistine to fight with him; for you are but a youth…"* (1 Samuel 17:33). When he came to fight, Goliath dismissed him on account of his youth: *"When the Philistine looked and saw David, he disdained him; for he was but a youth…"* (1 Samuel 17:42). David was not even supposed to be there, as was bluntly pointed out by his oldest brother Eliab (1 Samuel 17:28).

Second, David was not adequately trained and equipped (at least not from a human perspective). Saul contrasted David – *"a youth"* – with Goliath – *"a warrior from youth"* (1 Samuel 17:33) – implying that David had no training to fight in battle. Besides being untrained, he had no armor and no suitable weapon of war (1 Samuel 17:38-39). Instead, he faced the giant with a stick, five stones, and a sling (1 Samuel 17:40).

Third, David's opponent was a warrior and a giant. We already noticed how Goliath had been trained as *"a warrior from his youth"* (1 Samuel 17:33). If his training was not enough to intimidate any potential opponent, Goliath's size – a height of *"six cubits and a span"* (1 Samuel 17:4), which was about nine and a half feet tall – would have deterred almost anyone.

Fourth, David's opponent was an enemy of God. Of course, to David, this only served as further motivation to fight (1 Samuel 17:26, 36, 45-47). But this was more than just a physical fight. David had to stand up and fight in the name of God against an opponent who was bold enough that he *"taunted the armies of the living God"* (1 Samuel 17:36).

David Took Courage

David knew what was right. He knew that this enemy of God had to be defeated (1 Samuel 17:36).

David recognized the reward, both for himself and for the nation of Israel. He would receive riches and the king's daughter in marriage (1 Samuel 17:25). More importantly, the Israelites would defeat and plunder their enemy (1 Samuel 17:46, 52-53).

Finally, David took action. He did not wait to be called upon; he volunteered (1 Samuel 17:32). When Goliath ridiculed him, he boldly answered (1 Samuel 17:45-46). When the time came to fight, David did not hesitate, but *"ran quickly toward the battle line"* and killed the giant (1 Samuel 17:48-49).

Application for Us

There are a few lessons we should take from the example of David.

First, we must have courage to fight, no matter who we are. Paul wrote to the Corinthians about *"our warfare"* (2 Corinthians 10:4). Participation in the spiritual battle that will continue to be waged until the Lord returns is not only for a select few. All must be willing to fight. Youth does not make one exempt. Paul told Timothy, *"Let no one look down on your youthfulness, but...show yourself an example of those who believe"* (1 Timothy 4:12). Youth is no excuse for failing to do what God has called His people to do.

Second, we must not worry about being adequately equipped. Peter and John were seen as *"uneducated and untrained men,"* yet they displayed great boldness in proclaiming Christ (Acts 4:12-13). We may also be *"uneducated and untrained"* by the world's standard, but we are adequately prepared for our fight when we put on the armor that God provides (Ephesians 6:14-17).

Third, we must not worry about who our opponents are. Paul said, *"Put on the full armor of God, so that you will be able to stand firm against the schemes of the devil. For our struggle is not against flesh and blood, but against the rulers, against the powers, against the world forces of this darkness, against the spiritual forces of wickedness in the heavenly places"* (Ephesians 6:11-12). We have some powerful opponents against us. But we must remember that Christ is over all of them (Ephesians 1:20-21) and that through Him we will be victorious (Revelation 17:14).

Fourth, we must direct our fight against those who are the enemies of God. *"We do not war according to the flesh"* (2 Corinthians 10:3) because our fight is spiritual in nature. We fight to destroy *"speculations and every lofty thing raised up against the knowledge of God"* (2 Corinthians 10:5).

Conclusion

David was confident that the Lord would be with him. He told Goliath, *"This day the Lord will deliver you up into my hands, and I will strike you down and remove your head from you...for the battle is the Lord's and He will give you into our hands"* (1 Samuel 17:46-47). We must be confident as well. Though powerful forces *"will wage war against the Lamb...the Lamb will overcome them, because He is Lord of lords and King of kings"* (Revelation 17:14). Therefore, let us *take courage* and *"contend earnestly for the faith"* (Jude 3). Let us *"fight the good fight of faith"* (1 Timothy 6:12) so that we can share in the Lord's victory as He triumphs in the end.

Questions for Discussion & Reflection

1. Are young Christians exempt from fighting the good fight of faith? Explain.

2. Why might the world view us as being unqualified to defend the truth?

3. How do we equip ourselves for the spiritual warfare in which we are to be engaged?

4. Against whom is our struggle?

5. Explain why we are able to be confident that we will be victorious.

6. Rather than warring according to the flesh, explain how Christians are to do battle for the cause of the Lord.

Amos

The Courage to Speak Out

Amos may be the one in our series with whom people are most unfamiliar. Yet his is a powerful example of one who had the courage to speak out – to proclaim the truth *and* condemn error.

> "Then Amaziah, the priest of Bethel, sent word to Jeroboam king of Israel, saying, 'Amos has conspired against you in the midst of the house of Israel; the land is unable to endure all his words. For thus Amos says, "Jeroboam will die by the sword and Israel will certainly go from its land into exile"' Then Amaziah said to Amos, 'Go, you seer, flee away to the land of Judah and there eat bread and there do your prophesying! But no longer prophesy at Bethel, for it is a sanctuary of the king and a royal residence.'
>
> "Then Amos replied to Amaziah, 'I am not a prophet, nor am I the son of a prophet; for I am a herdsman and a grower of sycamore figs. But the Lord took me from following the flock and the Lord said to me, "Go prophesy to My people Israel"'" (Amos 7:10-15).

It is not always easy to speak out when the truth is unpopular and unwelcome. This is the situation in which we often find ourselves today. It was also the situation for the prophet Amos. If we are to have the courage to speak out today, we would do well to remember the example of Amos.

The Background

Amos described himself as "*a herdsmen*" (Amos 7:14). He was "*among the sheepherders from Tekoa*" (Amos 1:1) – a relatively insignificant village of Judah at the edge of the wilderness. Though he was from Judah, God sent him to prophesy primarily to the tribes of Israel (Amos 3:1; 4:1; 5:1; 7:8-9; 8:1-2; *et al.*).

Amos also said that he was "*not a prophet*" (Amos 7:14). Of course, he was a prophet in the sense that he spoke from God (Amos 7:15), but he was not a prophet *by profession*. In that time, prophets were often employed by rulers, such as the "*450 prophets of Baal and 400 prophets of the Asherah, who* [ate] *at Jezebel's table*" (1 Kings 18:19). Amos did not make his living this way. Instead, he provided for himself in his work as a herdsman.

Amos was also not the "*son of a prophet*" (Amos 7:14). He was not referring to the fact that his father was not a prophet. He was referring instead to what we might call the "schools" of the prophets where they would be trained to do the work. The "*sons of the prophets*" trained under an older prophet (cf. 2 Kings 2:15; 4:1). Amos did not receive such training.

Amos also prophesied during "*the days of Jeroboam son of Joash, king of Israel*" (Amos 1:1; cf. 2 Kings 14:23-29). Jeroboam "*did evil in the sight of the Lord*" (2 Kings 14:24), yet the nation enjoyed a degree of success during his reign

(2 Kings 14:25, 28). This was done, not by the might of Jeroboam, but by the will of God (2 Kings 14:26-27). But the nation had been blessed, compared to former years, while a wicked king ruled over them. It is often difficult to find support in criticizing a ruler during such times of economic or military success. Yet this was the position in which Amos found himself.

Why This Took Courage

Let us notice five reasons why it took *courage* for Amos to speak out in the way that he did.

First, Amos' message was against everyone. We sometimes hear the phrase, "the enemy of my enemy is my friend." This suggests that we can often find support from the enemies of those whom we criticize. Paul used this tactic to his advantage as he briefly won the support of the Pharisees against the Sadducees (Acts 23:6-10). Yet Amos would have no such allies. His message would have made him the "enemy" of all. He condemned the surrounding nations (Amos 1:3, 6, 9, 11, 13; 2:1). He condemned his home nation of Judah (Amos 2:4). He also condemned the nation to which he was sent – Israel (Amos 2:6-8; 3:1). Amos would have no allies among these nations.

Second, Amos' message was not "politically correct." He would have offended certain people, particularly those he referred to as the *"cows of Bashan"* (Amos 4:1).

Third, Amos' message was not his preference. When God showed him visions that signified the destruction of the people, he protested: *"Lord God, please pardon! How can Jacob stand, for he is small?"* (Amos 7:2; cf. 7:4). He did not want the prophecies to be true. But eventually he could no longer protest. Once God introduced "*a plumb line*" into the vision (Amos 7:7-8) – a clear, fixed standard – Amos understood why God was right to punish the people that the prophet first hoped would be spared.

Fourth, Amos' message was unwelcome. Amaziah made it clear that Amos was not welcome there: "*Go, you seer, flee away to the land of Judah... But no longer prophesy at Bethel, for it is a sanctuary of the king and a royal residence*" (Amos 7:13).

Fifth, Amos' work of prophesying was uncompensated. Amaziah suggested that Amos go to Judah "*and there eat bread and there do your prophesying*" (Amos 7:12), implying that he needed to go to Judah if he hoped to be compensated for his work in prophesying because there would be no such support in Israel. Yet Amos was not a prophet because he received support (Amos 7:14). He did the work even though he received no financial compensation for it.

Amos Took Courage

Amos knew what was right. Being a prophet in the literal sense, he received the word of God directly from the Holy Spirit (2 Peter 1:20-21).

Amos believed it was better for him to serve the Lord than to enjoy the benefits of serving a wicked king. If he simply prophesied what Jeroboam would have liked to hear, he may have been able to "*eat bread*" at his table (Amos 7:12; cf. 1 Kings 18:19). But he chose instead to be faithful to the Lord and reveal His message without compromise.

Finally, Amos took courage and spoke out. Without any formal training or compensation, he went out to prophesy. It was not because he had nothing else to do – he could have stayed plenty busy in his work as a herdsman without also doing the work of a prophet. But he went because God called him to go (Amos 7:15).

Application for Us

Even though we will not be personally called by God and given a message directly from the Holy Spirit, we can certainly make applications from Amos' example.

First, we must remember that our message is against everyone. Or course, in reality, the gospel we preach is *for* everyone (Mark 16:15; Acts 10:34-35). But it will be *perceived* as being *against* everyone – against the *atheists* because we affirm that it is *"the fool"* who says, *"There is no God"* (Psalm 14:1; cf. Romans 1:20); against the *world religions* because we declare that salvation is only in Christ (Acts 4:12); against the *denominations* because we teach that there is just *one* church (Matthew 16:18), and that every church of man will be *"uprooted"* (Matthew 15:13); and against our *erring brethren* because we implore the ones who have *"left* [their] *first love"* and have become *"dead"* to return to the Lord (Revelation 2:4; 3:1), follow the New Testament pattern (2 Timothy 1:13), and do everything by the authority of Christ (Colossians 3:17). Though our message may not be popular, *"we cannot stop speaking"* about the word of God (Acts 4:20).

Second, our message will not be seen as being "politically correct." Probably the most notable example of not being "politically correct" is teaching what the Bible says about homosexuality – that it is unnatural, indecent, and error (Romans 1:26-27); it is unrighteous and will keep one out of the kingdom of God (1 Corinthians 6:9-10); and it is "*contrary to sound teaching*" (1 Timothy 1:10). Many will be offended by one who teaches these things – even some in the religious world. But we must teach "*the whole counsel of God*" (Acts 20:27, NKJV), even if it is offensive to some.

Third, our message may not be our preference. It might be nice to believe that salvation could be by faith alone or that once one is saved, he cannot be lost. We could believe in the eternal security of more of our friends and family that way. But these ideas are contrary to the word of God (James 2:24; Hebrews 4:11; *et al.*). We must "*speak as the oracles of God*" (1 Peter 4:11, NKJV). Our way is not better than God's (Proverbs 14:12).

Fourth, our message is often unwelcome. Many will not want to hear what we have to say. Paul said, "*For am I now seeking the favor of men, or of God? Or am I striving to please men? If I were still trying to please men, I would not be a bond-servant of Christ*" (Galatians 1:10). We need to remember that the message of the gospel is not designed to *please* men, but to *save* men (Romans 1:16).

Fifth, we must not speak out in the hopes of obtaining some financial gain. Even for those who dedicate their lives to the preaching of the gospel, while it is right for them to "*get their living from the gospel*" (1 Corinthians 9:14), they may not always receive such support (1 Corinthians 9:6, 12, 18). But regardless of whether one is a gospel preacher or a Christian teaching his friends, family, or co-workers, we should not be motivated by the hope of gaining something in this life. Instead, we are to "*store up...treasures in heaven*" (Matthew 6:20) and "*press on toward the goal for the prize of the upward call of God in Christ Jesus*" (Philippians 3:14). We strive to "*persuade men*," not to receive some material reward, but to help prepare as many as we can for their appointment "*before the judgment seat of Christ*" (2 Corinthians 5:10-11).

Conclusion

Though he had a message that was offensive and unwelcome, Amos spoke out. Despite the fact that he had no allies and no financial support to ease his burden, Amos spoke out. And even though God called him to deliver a message of judgment that he wished himself was not true, Amos spoke out. Let us learn from the example of the prophet Amos so that we will also have the courage to speak out, no matter what the consequences might be.

Questions for Discussion & Reflection

1. What is the significance of the prophet Amos saying, "*I am not a prophet*"?

2. When we speak the truth, in what way is our message against everyone?

3. What are some "politically incorrect" truths we must proclaim?

4. Is truth based upon our preference? Explain.

5. In preaching the gospel, explain the difference between *pleasing* men and *saving* men.

6. Explain how the hope of financial gain can cause a preacher to compromise the truth.

Josiah

The Courage to Restore

A restoration took place in the days of Josiah, king of Judah. He sought to *restore* the practices of the Law of Moses that had been abandoned.

> *"Then the king sent, and they gathered to him all the elders of Judah and of Jerusalem. The king went up to the house of the Lord and all the men of Judah and all the inhabitants of Jerusalem with him, and the priests and the prophets and all the people, both small and great; and he read in their hearing all the words of the book of the covenant which was found in the house of the Lord.*

> *"The king stood by the pillar and made a covenant before the Lord, to walk after the Lord, and to keep His commandments and His testimonies and His statutes with all his heart and all his soul, to carry out the words of this covenant that were written in this book. And all the people entered into the covenant"* (2 Kings 23:1-3).

An effort began in the 19th century in this country to *restore* the New Testament church. We often refer to this effort as the Restoration Movement. It was a call for people to leave the churches of men and forsake the creeds of men.

The restorers encouraged people to follow the Scriptures as their only rule of faith and practice, then unite upon the word of God alone. It is not easy to give up what one has been taught or to leave those with whom one has had fellowship. But many did. Josiah's example helps us see how we can have the courage to restore whatever may be lacking in our service to God.

The Background

Josiah became king when he was just eight years old (2 Kings 22:1). What would have to happen to make a boy king? It would take some unusual circumstances. First, his father was assassinated (2 Kings 21:23). Then the people, rather than submitting to the would-be usurpers of the throne, rebelled against the conspirators, killed them, and made the young son of Amon king in his place (2 Kings 21:24).

Josiah did not have an ideal upbringing. Besides the fact that his father was killed by the time he was eight years old, his father *did evil in the sight of the Lord*" (2 Kings 21:20-22). His grandfather, Manasseh, was exceedingly wicked – even to the point of sacrificing his son as a burnt offering to a pagan god (2 Kings 21:2-6). He was so evil that despite his grandson Josiah's reforms, God still destroyed Judah *because of all the provocations with which Manasseh had provoked Him*" (2 Kings 23:26). Josiah did not have the type of upbringing that would tend to produce faithfulness at such a young age.

Despite all of this, Josiah had a good heart. He was interested in spiritual things, which led him to repair the Lord's house (2 Kings 22:3-7). His tender heart made him receptive to the word of God and inclined to obey it (2 Kings 22:19; 23:25).

However, the nation had departed far from the truth. The book of the law had been lost (2 Kings 22:8-10) and, therefore, had not been kept (2 Kings 22:13). The Passover had to be re-instituted (2 Kings 23:21-23). The idols, mediums, and spiritists had to be removed from the land (2 Kings 23:24). Sin and immorality were widespread – including the presence of "*male cult prostitutes*" and child sacrifices (2 Kings 23:7, 10).

Why This Took Courage

The nation had a long way to go to return to the Lord and His ways. Because of this, Josiah needed *courage* to restore the practices God commanded and the purity He demanded of His people.

First, Josiah needed to change. Though one could easily argue that Josiah was better than most of the others, he needed to return to the Lord as well. The book of God's law had been lost (2 Kings 22:8-10). Therefore, he – as well as the nation as a whole – needed to correct the sins they had been committing in ignorance.

Second, Josiah had to combat tradition. By the time the book of the law was found, the erroneous practices that existed in the land had been going on for a while – some dated back to the reign of Solomon (2 Kings 23:13). It is often difficult to combat tradition – even when it is wrong – because people become accustomed to it and learn to tolerate it.

Third, Josiah had to go against what his family had done. Both his father and his grandfather were evil men (2 Kings 21:1-2, 19-20). Rather than following in their footsteps, he needed to observe their sins and "*not do likewise*" (Ezekiel 18:14).

Fourth, Josiah had to oppose the errorists. This was not just about Josiah making up his own mind to change his life. He had to mount a *real* opposition against *real* people. Truth is often easier to accept in theory than in practice – particularly when it comes to opposing those who are the enemies of the truth.

Fifth, Josiah had to submit to a higher law. He was the king, but he was not above the law – especially God's law. Some rulers believe they are the ultimate authority. But Josiah recognized his responsibility to do what all must do – obey God (cf. Psalm 72:11).

Josiah Took Courage

Josiah knew what was right. After the book of the law was found, Shaphan the scribe "*read it in the presence of the king*" (2 Kings 22:10).

Josiah understood the benefit of restoring the practices of God's law. Upon hearing the words of the law, Josiah recognized the state of the nation: "*For great is the wrath of the Lord that burns against us, because our fathers have not listened to the words of this book, to do according to all that is written concerning us*" (2 Kings 22:13). The law of God contained blessings for obedience and curses for disobedience (Deuteronomy 28). He knew it would be better for the people to serve the Lord and receive His blessings.

After learning the truth, Josiah acted. He *"made a covenant"* to keep the law (2 Kings 23:3), then obeyed the law and carried out the necessary reforms. *"Before him there was no king like him who turned to the Lord with all his heart and with all his soul and with all his might, according to all the law of Moses; nor did any like him arise after him"* (2 Kings 23:25).

Application for Us

As we seek to restore (or maintain) faithful service to God, we should learn from Josiah's example.

First, we must be willing to change when necessary. No one is perfect. Paul reminded us of this when he said, *"All have sinned and fall short of the glory of God"* (Romans 3:23). Even Christians can be wrong, as Peter (Cephas) *"stood condemned"* for his sin (Galatians 2:11). When we are wrong, we need to repent – whether that means repudiating sin in our individual lives (Acts 8:20-22) or correcting errors in the congregation with which we worship (Revelation 2:4-5).

Second, we must not allow ourselves to be enslaved to tradition. Though the word *tradition* in regard to religious matters carries an immediate negative connotation with some, not all traditions are wrong. Paul told the brethren in Thessalonica: *"Stand firm and hold to the traditions which you were taught, whether by word of mouth, or by letter from us"* (2 Thessalonians 2:15). But we must abandon the traditions of men that are contrary to the law of God (Matthew 15:6-9) –

no matter how long we or those before us held the tradition.

Third, we must not place family above our service to God. The Lord must come first in all things. Jesus said, "*He who loves father or mother more than Me is not worthy of Me; and he who loves son or daughter more than Me is not worthy of Me*" (Matthew 10:37). Following Christ will sometimes put us at odds with those who are closest to us in this life. It is difficult to see these ties threatened. But it is far worse to be "*severed from Christ*," as this means we have "*fallen from grace*" (Galatians 5:4).

Fourth, we must be willing to oppose error. This means we must oppose those who *promote* error: "*Keep your eye on those who cause dissensions and hindrances contrary to the teaching which you learned, and turn away from them*" (Romans 16:17). It also means we must oppose those who *practice* error: "*Now we command you, brethren, in the name of our Lord Jesus Christ, that you keep away from every brother who leads an unruly life and not according to the tradition which you received from us*" (2 Thessalonians 3:6). Many prefer the path of compromise in their attempt to be more tolerant than God. Because of this, we will often face opposition, not just from the errorists, but from weak-kneed brethren who sympathize with them.

Fifth, we must submit to a higher law. King Josiah was certainly not exempt from God's law. We are not either. Jesus has "*all authority*" (Matthew 28:18). Therefore, we must "*do all in the name of the Lord*" (Colossians 3:17). He will save "*all those who obey Him*" (Hebrews 5:9). So we must be sure we measure up to His standard of judgment (John 12:48).

Conclusion

When Josiah found the book of the law of God and discovered that the nation was not keeping His commandments, he could have chosen to ignore it. He could have given preference to tradition, family ties, and the contrived harmony that comes through religious compromise. Instead, he chose to side with God and restore the practices and purity of service according to His law. We must have the courage that Josiah had to look honestly and humbly at the word of God. If we find we have fallen short in certain areas, we must make whatever corrections are necessary. If we are following the divine pattern in other areas, we must maintain our faithful service and not *"turn aside to the right or to the left"* (2 Kings 22:2).

Questions for Discussion & Reflection

1. In regard to spiritual practices, when would a restoration be necessary?

2. Are all traditions wrong? Explain.

3. How can we become enslaved to tradition?

4. Why must error be opposed?

5. When we oppose error, who will often oppose us (besides the errorists)?

6. What is the authority to which we are to submit?

Shadrach, Meshach, and Abed-nego
The Courage to Trust in God

The example of Shadrach, Meshach, and Abed-nego shows us the courage needed to put one's complete trust in God. Of course, other men in the examples we have already noticed have trusted in God, but the example of Daniel's friends is different – they did not receive special, direct revelation (as least not as far as we are told in the Scriptures) like many other Old Testament characters. Therefore, their example is very helpful for us today.

> "'*Now if you are ready, at the moment you hear the sound of the horn, flute, lyre, trigon, psaltery and bagpipe and all kinds of music, to fall down and worship the image that I have made, very well. But if you do not worship, you will immediately be cast into the midst of a furnace of blazing fire; and what god is there who can deliver you out of my hands?'*

> "*Shadrach, Meshach and Abed-nego replied to the king, 'O Nebuchadnezzar, we do not need to give you an answer concerning this matter. If it be so, our God whom we serve is able to deliver us from the furnace of blazing fire; and He will deliver us out of your hand, O king. But even if He does not, let it be known to you, O king, that we are not going to serve your gods*

or worship the golden image that you have set up" (Daniel 3:15-18).

We are called to trust God and be faithful to Him, even though our future in this life is uncertain. While we understand that God has the power to do a great many things (Ephesians 3:20), we must not think that He has some obligation to arrange events to turn out the way that *we* desire. Because of this, we must have *courage* to trust in God, even though He may allow us to suffer. This was the type of courage displayed by Shadrach, Meshach, and Abed-nego.

The Background

This took place during the time of the Babylonian captivity. When King Nebuchadnezzar came to Jerusalem, he took certain young men to be trained to serve in his court (Daniel 1:3-5). Among these youths were Daniel, Hananiah, Mishael, and Azariah (Daniel 1:6). The last three are better known by the names that were assigned to them: Shadrach, Meshach, and Abed-nego (Daniel 1:7). It is important to know *why* this happened. The text says, *"The Lord gave* [them] *into his hand"* (Daniel 1:2). This was done because of the sins of the nation (2 Kings 21:10-15; 23:27; 24:1-4). So it was not an accident, coincidence, or bad luck that this happened. It had been orchestrated by God.

These three were blessed by God, but lacked the ability to understand *"all kinds of visions and dreams"* like Daniel was able to do (Daniel 1:17). But they *"entered the king's personal service"* (Daniel 1:19). While serving the king, trouble came. The king made a golden statue and ordered all to worship it at the prescribed times (Daniel 3:1-5). The penalty for not worshipping the image was to be *"cast into the midst of a furnace of blazing fire"* (Daniel 3:6). When it was reported to Nebuchadnezzar that these three did not worship the image, he called them before him to answer (Daniel 3:12-14). He even gave them a second chance (Daniel 3:15); but they refused to comply, citing their trust in God (Daniel 3:16-18).

After this, Nebuchadnezzar heated the furnace seven times more than usual and threw in the three young men (Daniel 3:19-24). The furnace was so hot that even the guards who cast them in were killed themselves (Daniel 3:22). But Shadrach, Meshach, and Abed-nego survived (Daniel 3:24-25). When the king ordered them to come out, he found no injury, damage, or smell of fire on them (Daniel 3:26-27). Nebuchadnezzar responded by praising God for delivering these men and praising them for trusting in Him (Daniel 3:28-30).

Why This Took Courage

The Scriptures show as at least three reasons why the actions of Shadrach, Meshach, and Abed-nego took courage. [*For this study, we will ignore one reason – they had to defy the law – because this is the primary focus in our next example, Daniel.*]

First, they were among the few who did not worship the image (Daniel 3:12). This made them a target, as they were singled out and called before an angry king (Daniel 3:13). Most people prefer not to stir up trouble for themselves if they can help it.

Second, they had a second chance. When these three came before Nebuchadnezzar, the king gave them one more chance to comply with his order regarding the golden image (Daniel 3:15). This is common with persecution. Rulers will often rather spare one who is willing to denounce God than to kill one who serves God. Sadly, when given a second chance to sin, compromise, or deny the Lord, many are willing to take it.

Third, they did not know what would happen. They knew that God had the power to save them ("*Our God whom we serve is able to deliver us*" – Daniel 3:17); but they did not know that He would ("*But even if He does not...*" – Daniel 3:18). Again, they were not prophets like Daniel (Daniel 1:17); they had no way to know what was in store for them.

Shadrach, Meshach, and Abed-nego Took Courage

They knew what was right. Their refusal to worship the image was not rooted in youthful rebellion, but in submission to God and His commandment: "*You shall have no other gods before Me*" (Exodus 20:3).

They understood that there was a reward for refusing to worship this image. "*You shall not worship them or serve them; for I, the Lord your God, am a jealous God, visiting the iniquity of the fathers on the children... but showing lovingkindness to thousands, to those who love Me and keep My commandments*" (Exodus 20:5-6).

Finally, they acted, refusing to worship the image regardless of the consequences. They put their trust in God, even though they did not know what would happen.

Application for Us

As we face an uncertain future, we must learn a few lessons from the example of Shadrach, Meshach, and Abed-nego.

First, we must trust in God, even if we become a target. The Hebrew writer quoted from the Psalms when he wrote, *"The Lord is my helper, I will not be afraid. What will man do to me?"* (Hebrews 13:6; cf. Psalm 118:6). In reality, man can do many things to harm us. The Hebrew writer listed some of the experiences of these brethren earlier in his epistle: *"But remember the former days, when, after being enlightened, you endured a great conflict of sufferings, partly by being made a public spectacle through reproaches and tribulations, and partly by becoming sharers with those who were so treated"* (Hebrews 10:32-33). We may even have to face physical death (Revelation 2:10). But even if we are targeted and *"considered as sheep to be slaughtered...we overwhelmingly conquer through Him who loved us"* (Romans 8:36-37). Even if we are singled out for persecution, we can still hope in the Lord.

Second, we must beware of "second chances" to sin, compromise, or deny the Lord. God has promised a *"way of escape"* for every *temptation* (1 Corinthians 10:13). But He has not promised a similar way of escape for every *persecution* (2 Timothy 3:12). We should not view a second chance to sin, compromise, or deny the Lord as a legitimate way to escape persecution. We must obey the Lord and stand for what is right, regardless of the consequences.

Third, we must trust in God, even if our future is uncertain. God may have the power to do something, but that does not mean that He will do it. His will is not the same as ours. "'For My thoughts are not your thoughts, nor are your ways My ways,' declares the Lord. 'For as the heavens are higher than the earth, so are My ways higher than your ways and My thoughts than your thoughts'" (Isaiah 55:8-9). Even when we pray, we must recognize that *His* will is what will be done (1 John 5:14-15). We must have faith in God no matter what lies ahead. The Christians in Smyrna were told that they were going to face imprisonment, tribulation, and death (Revelation 2:10). The Lord did not tell them that if they hoped and prayed fervently enough, that they could be assured of a deliverance from their persecution. Instead, they simply needed to be *"faithful until death."* Sadly, some lose their faith in God when He allows them to suffer in this life. It is important to remember the basis of true faith: *"Faith comes from hearing, and hearing by the word of Christ"* (Romans 10:17). Faith is not to be based upon God doing what we want Him to do. Our future is uncertain, but our faith in the Lord must be firmly anchored and steadfast (Hebrews 6:19).

Conclusion

Shadrach, Meshach, and Abed-nego were faced with the threat of death. They knew God had the power to deliver them but did not know if He would choose to do so. Despite this uncertainty, they placed their trust in God and were delivered. In the same way, we may be faced with threats and attacks today. We know that God has the power to deliver us and prevent us from suffering harm, but we do not know what will happen in our future. Rather than basing our faith upon God causing circumstances to unfold a certain way in our lives, we must base our faith upon His word. In the end, He will deliver us. Sure, we may have to face imprisonment, violence, and even death; but if we are faithful, He will still reward us with *"the crown of life"* (Revelation 2:10).

Questions for Discussion & Reflection

1. Why did Shadrach, Meshach, and Abed-nego refuse to worship the king's golden image?

2. Though these three were blessed by God along with Daniel, what advantage did Daniel have over them? (See Daniel 1:17)

3. Why do Christians face persecution?

4. When we face persecution, how can we do so without fear?

5. Why are "second chances" to sin so tempting?

6. Explain how faith can be maintained, despite an uncertain future.

Daniel

The Courage to Defy the Law

The final example in our study is Daniel. This lesson will focus on the courage he demonstrated in his willingness to violate the laws of men in order to be faithful to the Lord.

> "Then these commissioners and satraps came by agreement to the king and spoke to him as follows: 'King Darius, live forever! All the commissioners of the kingdom, the prefects and the satraps, the high officials and the governors have consulted together that the king should establish a statute and enforce an injunction that anyone who makes a petition to any god or man besides you, O king, for thirty days, shall be cast into the lions' den. Now, O king, establish the injunction and sign the document so that it may not be changed, according to the law of the Medes and Persians, which may not be revoked.' Therefore King Darius signed the document, that is, the injunction.

> "Now when Daniel knew that the document was signed, he entered his house (now in his roof chamber he had windows open toward Jerusalem); and he continued kneeling on his knees three times a day, praying and giving

thanks before his God, as he had been doing previously" (Daniel 6:6-10).

Persecution, in some form, is a certainty for Christians (2 Timothy 3:12; 1 Peter 4:12). Often the severest persecution will come from civil authorities. This can be carried out in one of two ways – either there will be evil rulers targeting Christians or there will be evil men with influence over unprincipled and/or ignorant lawmakers that will manipulate the rulers into targeting Christians. There are times in which Christians need to defy the law and suffer persecution in order to remain faithful to God. Peter famously said, *"We must obey God rather than men"* (Acts 5:29). Christians have generally enjoyed peace in this country. But as more evil men gain power and influence, our days of peace and freedom may be numbered. We need to be prepared to disobey the civil authorities if such becomes necessary in order to remain faithful to God. Daniel's example shows one with the courage to defy the law when it became necessary to do so.

The Background

Like the three men in our previous lesson, Daniel was taken from his home as a young man and served in Nebuchadnezzar's court (Daniel 1:3-7, 18-19; 2:48-49). While serving the Babylonian king, Daniel prophesied and affirmed the superiority of God's kingdom over every human kingdom (Daniel 2:31-45). Also during the days of this king, Nebuchadnezzar was made to live like a beast (Daniel 4:23-25, 28-33) in order to teach him that God was *"ruler over the realm of mankind"* (Daniel 4:17, 26, 34-37).

When his son Belshazzar came to power, the new king saw the writing on the wall during a feast and wanted someone to interpret it (Daniel 5:1-7). Daniel would interpret, but he first reminded Belshazzar that all authority is from God (Daniel 5:18) and that God reigns supreme over every human ruler (Daniel 5:21). Daniel then interpreted the handwriting, explaining to Belshazzar that the king was subject to God, had been judged by God, and would be punished by God (Daniel 5:25-28). Sure enough, *"that same night Belshazzar the Chaldean king was slain. So Darius the Mede received the kingdom"* (Daniel 5:30-31).

Daniel then served Darius and the king was pleased with him (Daniel 6:1-3). However, some were jealous and conspired against Daniel (Daniel 6:4). Knowing his character, they understood that the only way to trap him was to make his religion illegal (Daniel 6:5). So they crafted a piece of legislation that would make Daniel's religious practices against the law and convinced the king to sign it (Daniel 6:6-9).

Daniel knew that the law was signed and disobeyed it anyway, refusing to alter his service to God to conform to an ungodly decree. *"Now when Daniel knew that the document was signed, he entered his house (now in his roof chamber he had windows open toward Jerusalem); and he continued kneeling on his knees three times a day, praying and giving thanks before his God, as he had been doing previously"* (Daniel 6:10). When his enemies reported his defiance to the king, Darius tried unsuccessfully to rescue him (Daniel 6:11-15). After Daniel was cast into the lion's den (Daniel 6:16-18), Darius found him still alive in the morning (Daniel 6:19-22). Daniel was delivered from the den and his accusers were cast in and *"they had not reached the bottom of the den before the lions overpowered them and crushed all their bones"* (Daniel 6:23-24). Darius learned from this event and issued a decree recognizing the greatness and supremacy of God (Daniel 6:26-27).

Why This Took Courage

Let us consider five reasons why it took courage for Daniel to defy the law on this occasion.

First, he knew that the law was signed. This was not a law he violated in ignorance, which could have allowed him to plead for leniency when he was brought before the king. This was an act of deliberate defiance to the law.

Second, the penalty included "certain" death. Of course, death was only certain from a human perspective, ignoring the possibility of divine intervention. But it is interesting that Darius expressed confidence (or perhaps a hopeful desire) that God would deliver Daniel (Daniel 6:16), while nothing is mentioned about what Daniel thought would happen. We learned from the example of Shadrach, Meshach, and Abed-nego that God's people should have absolute faith in His power, but also recognize that God will not always act according to their desires. Daniel had to recognize that God could have allowed him to be killed in the lion's den.

Third, this was a short-term challenge. The law prohibiting men from petitioning *"any god or man"* besides the king would only be in force *"for thirty days"* (Daniel 6:7). Daniel could have reasoned that, rather than facing death for violating the law, it would be better for him to compromise his faith for thirty days and then return to serving God as he had previously done when law was expired.

Fourth, he did not go into hiding. Instead of closing his windows and trying to go unnoticed, Daniel kept the windows open while he prayed (Daniel 6:10). He could have tried to avoid trouble, but he did not.

Fifth, the king signed the law. Daniel had a good relationship with King Darius up to this point (Daniel 6:3). But even though the king did not write the law, he did sign it. There was no guarantee as to how he would react when he learned of Daniel's disobedience. He could have had sympathy for Daniel since the law was unfair (which he did); or he could have responded with anger for Daniel's open defiance to the law he signed (cf. Daniel 3:12-13, 19). Human reactions are often unpredictable as they are affected by a myriad of factors. Daniel chose to be faithful without regard to how King Darius would react.

Daniel Took Courage

Daniel knew what was right with regard to praying to God. When Solomon completed the temple, the Lord said, *"My people who are called by My name humble themselves and pray and seek My face and turn from their wicked ways, then I will hear from heaven, will forgive their sin and will heal their land"* (2 Chronicles 7:14). During this difficult time in the nation's history, Daniel continued to pray to God as the Lord expected His people to do.

Daniel also knew that being faithful to God and continuing to pray to Him was more important than conforming to an unjust human law. The forgiveness and healing that God promised (2 Chronicles 7:14) was worth far more than any favor from a human king.

Finally, Daniel took courage. When the law was signed, he did not procrastinate in hopes that the month might pass before he needed to take a stand. He prayed to God as he always had regardless of the consequences.

Application for Us

Since we never know when we may face persecution from the civil authorities for our faith, we need to learn from Daniel's example.

First, we should not hope to be able to claim ignorance. While it is sometimes true that those who are unaware of a law may get some leniency when they are caught, we must be faithful to God whether or not we are aware of a law that prohibits service to Him. When Peter and John were *"commanded...not to speak or teach at all in the name of Jesus,"* they said, *"We cannot stop speaking about what we have seen and heard"* (Acts 4:18-20). When they were arrested a second time, they said, *"We must obey God rather than men"* (Acts 5:29). They did not claim ignorance. They knew the law. But they willfully disobeyed it in order to carry out the will of the Lord.

Second, we must be faithful, even if punishment is certain. The Hebrew writer reminded his audience of some who *"were tortured, not accepting their release, so that they might obtain a better resurrection"* (Hebrews 11:35). Even if punishment is certain, we must endure it with joy (Acts 5:40-41) because of the reward that awaits us for our faithfulness (Matthew 5:11-12).

Third, we must not compromise "temporarily," thinking that the situation will improve later. First of all, the situation may not improve in the future. The wise man asked the question: *"If no one knows what will happen, who can tell him when it will happen?"* (Ecclesiastes 8:7). Situations that we think will be temporary may not be. Then, if we compromise, our unfaithfulness may end up being permanent. Furthermore, if we compromise our faith, we may not have time later to repent. Not only could we pass from this life at any time (Luke 12:19-20), but the Lord could return at any moment and call us before His judgment seat (2 Peter 3:10; 2 Corinthians 5:10). We cannot afford to risk the eternal fate of our souls for a "temporary" compromise.

Fourth, we must not be Christians in private only. Our faith must be visible to others. Jesus made this clear when He said, *"You are the light of the world. A city set on a hill cannot be hidden; nor does anyone light a lamp and put it under a basket, but on the lampstand, and it gives light to all who are in the house. Let your light shine before men in such a way that they may see your good works, and glorify your Father who is in heaven"* (Matthew 5:14-16).

Fifth, we must not worry about how others will react. When Peter and John were told by the Council not to preach anymore, they answered, *"Whether it is right in the sight of God to give heed to you rather than to God, you be the judge; for we cannot stop speaking about what we have seen and heard"* (Acts 4:19-20). They did not worry about how the men on the Council would react. They were determined to obey the Lord.

Conclusion

As society becomes more ungodly, persecution against Christians – particularly from the government – will become more common and more severe. Unless our country undergoes a significant change in direction, we must prepare for such persecution in our future. Daniel's deliberate defiance to the law of man in order to remain faithful to God is an example we need to remember today. No matter what laws may be passed, or what penalties may be imposed on Christians for following the Lord, we must always be willing to echo the words of Peter: *"We must obey God rather than men"* (Acts 5:29).

Questions for Discussion & Reflection

1. According to the Scriptures, explain the legitimate role of civil government.

2. How could a king who was pleased with Daniel sign a law that would cause him to be put to death?

3. Under what circumstances are we to willfully disobey civil law?

4. What do we hope to obtain by enduring persecution? (See Hebrews 11:35)

5. Explain why we must not compromise "temporarily" while we wait for conditions to improve.

6. Why is it important for others to know that we are Christians?

Courage Today

"Therefore, since we have so great a cloud of witnesses surrounding us, let us also lay aside every encumbrance and the sin which so easily entangles us, and let us run with endurance the race that is set before us, fixing our eyes on Jesus, the author and perfecter of faith, who for the joy set before Him endured the cross, despising the shame, and has sat down at the right hand of the throne of God. For consider Him who has endured such hostility by sinners against Himself, so that you will not grow weary and lose heart" (Hebrews 12:1-3).

The Hebrew writer mentioned the *"great cloud of witnesses,"* referring to the heroes of faith he had just discussed. Some of the examples we have considered in our study are in the list of the faithful in Hebrews 11. Because we have this *"great cloud of witnesses surrounding us,"* we must do three things:

1. Lay aside every encumbrance and sin, and run with endurance (Hebrews 12:1).
2. Look to Jesus and to His example (Hebrews 12:2).
3. Do not grow weary and lose heart (Hebrews 12:3).

In other words, *"take courage"* (John 16:33) – trust in the Lord and follow Him as He desires, no matter what the consequences might be.

The Purpose of This Study

We have spent several lessons looking at examples of courage. It is important that we know *why* we did this. It is not because these are good stories (though they are good stories – not mere legends or myths, however, but actual accounts). It is not so we can admire these men (though we ought to recognize their courage). It is not to provide some hollow motivation to make us feel good today but will be forgotten tomorrow.

The reason why we studied these examples of courage was so that *we will act with courage as well!* Courage is not just a characteristic of the "heroes" of faith – it is for *all* of us. This is why the Hebrew writer mentioned those "heroes" of faith – so the Hebrew Christians (as well as Christians today) would learn from their examples and then follow in the footsteps of Christ. We must *"not lose heart,"* but *"always* [be] *of good courage"* knowing the hope that awaits us following the trials of this life (2 Corinthians 4:16; 5:6).

The Foundation of Courage

The foundation of courage is *faith*. We cannot please God, nor can we display courage, without faith (Hebrews 11:6). The Hebrew writer mentioned the heroes of faith, as well as Jesus Himself, to admonish Christians to *"not grow weary and lose heart"* (Hebrews 12:3). Paul said we must be *"of good courage"* as we *"walk by faith, not by sight"* (2 Corinthians 5:6-7).

If we have trouble acting with courage, we need to examine our faith (cf. 2 Corinthians 13:5). Jude wrote about the need for Christians to build up their faith (Jude 20). How can we do this? He spoke earlier in his letter of the need to "*contend earnestly for the faith*" (Jude 3). How can we contend for the faith? We need to remember what Paul wrote: "*So faith comes from hearing, and hearing by the word of Christ*" (Romans 10:17). Faith is not miraculously given to us by God. Faith comes as we read, study, meditate, and practice the word. We must do this in order to equip ourselves to "*contend earnestly for the faith*" (Jude 3). We must also do this that we might build ourselves up on the foundation of faith (Jude 20).

How Do We Take Courage?

In the introduction to the study, we noticed *how* we can take courage. In each of our examples, we noticed how each of the men took these steps and demonstrated courage in their particular circumstances. We must also take these steps so that we might live with courage today.

We must know what is right – Many display courage in practicing and defending things that are wrong. While their courage is commendable, it is ultimately worthless if they are not standing for what is right. We must look to the Scriptures to find the truth (John 17:17; Psalm 119:160). While we are certainly able to understand the word of God (Ephesians 3:4), it will not come by accident or by some miracle. Instead, we must be committed to diligently studying the word of God so that we might learn how to handle it aright (2 Timothy 2:15).

We must know there is a reward – Once we know the truth, we need a reason to hold fast to it in the face of trials, opposition, temptation, and persecution. Without the hope of a reward, our lives are miserable (1 Corinthians 15:19). But we have hope through Christ (1 Corinthians 15:20; Hebrews 6:19). This should motivate us to do what we know to be right.

We must act – Courage is not just believing and being convinced of the truth. Ezra was admonished: *"Be courageous and act"* (Ezra 10:4). We must do the same.

Remember Our Examples

There are many examples of courage in the Bible that we could have considered. The eight we studied were chosen for a reason. They show us examples of ones who did what we must also be willing to do in our service to God today.

- **Abram: the courage to leave home** (Genesis 12:1, 4) – We must be willing to put God first over family (Matthew 10:37) and remember that we are just pilgrims here on the earth (1 Peter 2:11), lest we allow the people and things of this world to turn us away from the Lord.
- **Joseph: the courage to maintain purity** (Genesis 39:9) – We must *"flee from youthful lusts"* (2 Timothy 2:22), remembering that God sees all and that *"no creature is hidden from His sight"* (Hebrews 4:13). We must not think that we can compromise our purity and no one else will know. God knows.
- **Moses: the courage to lead** (Exodus 3:10) – Whether we find ourselves in some official

leadership position or not, we are to *"let* [our] *light shine"* so that we might point people to God (Matthew 5:14-16).

- **David: the courage to fight** (1 Samuel 17:45-46) – We are engaged in a spiritual war (2 Corinthians 10:3-4). Because of this, we must *"contend earnestly"* (Jude 3) as we *"fight the good fight of faith"* (1 Timothy 6:12).

- **Amos: the courage to speak out** (Amos 7:12-15) – We must always be ready to speak the truth (1 Peter 3:15) and do so in a way that represents the will of God accurately (1 Peter 4:11). Often such a defense of the truth will not be popular, but we cannot afford to worry about how others will react (Galatians 1:10).

- **Josiah: the courage to restore** (2 Kings 23:3, 25) – Instead of doing what we have always done or blindly following those around us, we must follow the pattern that has been revealed in the word of God (2 Timothy 1:13). We should respect Christ's authority enough that we *"do all in the name of the Lord Jesus"* (Colossians 3:17). If this necessitates a change in our beliefs or practices, we must be willing to make such a change.

- **Shadrach, Meshach, and Abed-nego: the courage to trust in God** (Daniel 3:16-18) – We do not know what the future holds. As the church in Smyrna was warned, we could also face imprisonment, tribulation, and death for our faith (Revelation 2:10). Regardless of what could happen, we must put our complete trust in God and *"be faithful until death"* (Revelation 2:10).

- **Daniel: the courage to defy the law** (Daniel 6:10) – The more that wicked people come into positions of power and influence, the more likely it will be for laws to be created for the purpose of targeting Christians. Even if our service to God is illegal, *"we must obey God rather than men"* (Acts 5:29).

Conclusion

The individuals in our study acted with courage. But they did not miraculously receive courage from the Lord. They learned what to do and why they should do it, then acted with courage and carried out the Lord's commands by their own free will. They could have chosen to compromise, but they did not. We will often be tempted to compromise our faith. Yet we must remain steadfast. In all of the challenges that we face, let us *take courage* and obey the Lord no matter what the consequences might be.

Questions for Discussion & Reflection

1. What does the Hebrew writer say we must do *"since we have so great a cloud of witnesses surrounding us"*?

2. Why are these examples important?

3. How does the example of Christ motivate us to *take courage*?

4. What is the foundation of courage?

5. How do we establish this foundation?

6. What are the three steps we must take in order to *take courage*?

Other Books by the Author

NEW – *Bringing Up Children in the Lord*
The topic of parenting is vital – not only for the Lord's church, but also for society as a whole. Children are the future; therefore, it is important that parents take their responsibility seriously to bring up their children in the right way. This book contains a 6-lesson study on the topic of parenting.

NEW – *Making Wise Investments: How to Gain an Everlasting Reward*
The Bible speaks of investments we are to make that are of a *spiritual* nature. While financial investments have their place, these spiritual investments are far more valuable and important than those that pertain to this life. This book contains 7 lessons about how to make wise investments in our spiritual lives.

My Son, Hear My Words: Notes on Proverbs
This book arranges the verses in Proverbs by topic and then provides commentary on the text. The commentary in this book is a valuable reference tool as you seek to learn and apply the teachings in the book of Proverbs. Its topical arrangement also makes it useful for personal and group Bible studies.

Daily Notes & Observations
This book contains 365 Scripture-based articles on a wide range of topics, taken from every area of the word of God. These articles, as well as the Bible reading plans and spaces for your notes, are designed to encourage a regular habit of studying and meditating upon the Scriptures.

For more information about these books, as well as other helpful materials, visit www.GospelArmory.com.

16227214R00053

Printed in Poland
by Amazon Fulfillment
Poland Sp. z o.o., Wrocław